John,
Enjoy,
Scott Lee

TRUE FISH STORIES AND OTHER LIES

VOLUME 1

BY

SCOTT LEE

Published in Tennessee

First Edition December 2012

Cover art and design by Dale Goodloe

Cover original watercolor by
Deborah Ezell-Denson

ISBN: 978-1480002432.

Printed in the United States of America

TABLE OF CONTENTS

SECTION 1
TRUE FISH STORIES

SECTION 2
OTHER LIES

TRUE FISH STORIES AND OTHER LIES is dedicated to the memory of Jackson Lee, "Uncle Frank" Lee, W.E. "Uncle Willie" Barrow and Lance Fielder.

Thank you, gentlemen, for your contributions to my life and to these stories. Rest in Peace.

It is also dedicated to my son, Travis, who continues to be one of my finest teachers.

Introduction

True Fish Stories and Other Lies:Volume 1 is a series of short stories many of which are about fishing. All of them are PG-13 or lighter and are true…or at least should be.

Many are designed to make you laugh. Others are written to touch the soft part of your heart as they touched mine. All are written to entertain.

It is my mission for you to doubt the true ones and believe the lies and I'll probably fool you with most of them.

I am working on *True Fish Stories and Other Lies: Volume 2*. If you have an original story you'd like me to publish, please email your story and your contact information to: Scott@SchoolhouseEarthBooks.com

I'm also working on *TRUE FLYING STORIES AND OTHER LIES: VOLUME 1* and am seeking contributors.

Opening Day

My dad was not a fisherman. He was not a hunter or a camper or a whitewater rafter or a canoe paddler. He was not an outdoorsman at all. He was a city boy and…he was a great father.

I became a fisherman on my birthday…my first birthday. I was born with it. Dad realized this by the time I was ten years old. At that time we were living in what I've heard called upstate New York. I guess "upstate" distinguishes it from "The City".

Not far from us was a world renowned trout stream known as Catherine Creek. Creek is pronounced crick, rhymes with brick, in Yankeeland. Down South the word rhymes with week, sleek, leak and sneak.

Also in Yankeeland they close fishing season for a time in the winter. I've always assumed it was to keep those who suffer from terminal cases of fishing pox from freezing to death.

Dad announced one evening at supper that he and I were going to fish Opening Day at Catherine Creek. The trip was planned for the next weekend and I was so elated that I was sure I wouldn't sleep at all until then.

That Friday we packed the station wagon with enough supplies for a battalion bivouac and headed out. An hour later we pulled over and pitched a pup tent. Mom's P B and J's were a big hit and we settled in for the night. It was cold as penguin poop that night but heavy sleeping bags and hoodies kept us cozy all night.

The next morning, just before first light, Dad started a fire. He was so not an outdoorsman that he cooked the eggs before cooking the bacon. I guess I don't have to describe the result.

At daybreak there were eleventy-seven shoulder to shoulder fishermen at the hole we'd planned to fish when we arrived and we couldn't even get a line into the water. We saw one guy hook a pretty good trout but it snagged about twenty other lines as it raced around the pool and finally got off. It took the assembled fishermen over an hour to untangle the lines and resume fishing. No one caught anything all day.

What I carry today from that experience is the recollection of a man who loved his son so much that he would try something he knew nothing about so that his boy could have a memory.

I'm exactly not sure what love is. I am sure that my father's actions that day were a direct result of the kind of love that Paul wrote about.

Rest in Peace, Jackson. You were a great Dad to me.

Bluegill

Camp Iroquois was on one of New York's Finger Lakes, Seneca, I think and it was the summer before third grade when I got the news that I was going for two weeks. Cabins full of bunk beds, chow hall with group tables, hot dogs and baked beans and loud farts, "bug juice" to drink, canoeing, hiking, camp fires, funny camp songs, capture the flag, scouts and raiders, teen-age counselors, starry nights and fishing from the dock; a small boy's dream come true.

My first fish was a bluegill about the size of my nine-year old hand. He and I got hooked at the same time. He on a worm baited cane-pole and me on fishing. He was released unharmed a few moments later. Sixty years later I'm still hooked.

I have always admired the bluegill's fight. Ounce for ounce they are the hardest fighting fish I've ever caught. A friend of mine says that if bluegills got as big as bass it wouldn't be safe to swim in fresh water. I think he's right.

The bluegill is known by several aliases: bream, sunfish, sunny, sun perch and by the complete novice, perch. There are several sub-species of bluegill in my native southland. The standard bluegill that most of the kids in Tennessee are familiar with is easy to find and easy to catch. Like all of his cousins he likes worms, crickets and small artificials.

The redbreast that my buddy Stumpy from Waycross, Georgia introduced me to in the Satilla River features a bright red or bright yellow belly and grows pretty big. Redbreasts over a pound are common in South Georgia where the growing season is over thirteen months a year.

The shell cracker aka warmouth has a standard bluegill's distinctive ear flap but has a magnificent turquoise lightning bolt on his cheeks and has a mouth more like a bass's than a bluegill's. He is the smallest of his clan but please don't mention it as he is very sensitive about his size. He likes to hide in deep cover and race out to hit small baits like a runaway train.

The Punkin' Seed is the flashiest dresser in his clan. Most folks comment on catching their first one that it looks like it belongs in salt water because of its' magnificent colors.

The Bluegill is a noble and benevolent species. I am personally acquainted with one that almost saved a very nice lady twenty-five years of frustration.

My first wife and I were married my senior year in college. Well, actually it was my second senior year. I'm not a quick study.

She used to love to tell the tale of one night when I was snoring and she tapped me on the shoulder and asked me to roll over.

According to her, I responded from my dream, "I can't, I'm watching the bobbers."

One Saturday afternoon I was fishing a farm pond near the campus. The drought had dropped the water to the lowest level I'd ever seen and two previously invisible stumps a foot or so apart could be seen a few inches under the surface. I dropped my popping bug between them. It hit the water and just kept going down.

I was sure it was a bass for the first five minutes of the fight. It turned out to be a bluegill that weighed two pounds two ounces on the post office scales. I'd carried it there in a bucket of water as I'd wanted an accurate weight on this monster.

It lived in our bathtub for two days and every guy I knew at school came to see it. I think she would have divorced me then if it had lived just one more day and saved herself many years of grief.

Fishing addicts aren't easy for Earthlings to live with.

If you're not a fisherman you're probably wondering why I wrote this as it may not seem to go anywhere in particular and isn't very cohesive. It wasn't supposed to be. It was written as a tribute to the creativity of The Great Angler Who provided us with the magnificent fish we call the Bluegill.

Fishing Withdrawal

It had been a long winter and by the middle of March my buddy Ron and I were in the advanced stages of fishing withdrawal. He had developed a tic over his left eye and I was having trouble speaking in complete sentences. Every real fisherman knows exactly what I'm talking about.

A few days before, we had gone to a tackle store in hopes of lessening our symptoms by doing what my daughter calls "fondling the plastic fish". In other words we had touched a bunch of fish related paraphernalia and bought some lures we didn't need.

My wife had stood behind us, shaking her head, as we filled the bathtub to see the new lures in action. This helped for a while but the fishing withdrawal symptoms returned a couple of days later.

The night of March 31 he called me around 8 o'clock, "Weatherman says tomorrow will be partly cloudy with a high in the early forties....wanna go?"

Silly question.

Around 9 AM the next morning we arrived at a favorite small stream where we had permission to park and fish. It took us a while to unload and dress. We were wearing long johns under lined jeans and heavy coats. It was not easy to pull the soft chest waders over that much clothing and we had to tie each other's boots as neither of us could bend over far enough to tie our own. Stocking caps and eye protection completed the outfits.

I paused to give thanks for the day in hopes that The Almighty would see that neither of us fell today as getting up would be a tough proposition.

As we donned wearable tackle boxes and grabbed our rods the snow began to fall...really fall. The flakes were about the size of my watch crystal and not very far apart. I'd guess the visibility was less than 300 yards.

"Perfect!" He said, "The fish will never expect us in this weather!"

I suppose there is a certain amount of anthropomorphism in all fishermen but I doubted that the fish were going to expect us, snow or not.

We stopped several times to knock the snow off of our boots before we finally stepped into the creek.

As we worked our way upstream I began to notice that the snowflakes were definitely coming faster and closer together. I was knee deep about 20 feet ahead of him, fishing a particularly long pool when a small snowball splashed down near my leg. I quickly looked back at my buddy but he was focused on his retrieve and appeared innocent. *"April Fools!"* I thought.

No way is he innocent! I have never seen a smallmouth bass throw a snowball and there were no other people around. I quickly refocused on my fishing and was soon the victim of another snowball near miss.

I figured out his MO. He was waiting until I was looking the other way and then throwing almost straight up to give himself time to go back to fishing and continue to feign innocence.

I decided to let him continue his little game. This was not the first time one of us had messed with the other one.

Like all of our favorite spots on this stream, this one produced nothing that day. A few minutes later he caught up to me and said, "Let's try a couple of more casts here and move on." He was still not letting on.

We had stood shoulder to shoulder for about 3 casts apiece when something splashed right in front of us. In unison we said, "I thought you were throwing snowballs at me!"

The flakes had gotten so big and so close together that the swirling wind was actually hooking them up into small balls in the air as they fell. We stood and watched the pool for a few minutes and saw many more snow balls splash down. By now the trees were covered and so was the ground. Our part of planet Earth had become a living Christmas Card. We stood in awe and just took it all in.

The snow fell for the whole six hours we fished and we only caught 2 fish all day. The same guy caught both of them but I'm not going to tell you which of us caught them because it doesn't matter. To me fishing isn't a competitive sport. It's a team sport. *We* caught 2.

This story is dedicated to those fishermen who understand that we caught two fish in six hours and it was one of the best days we ever had fishing.

Assumption is the Mother...

I've heard it said that the names have been changed to protect the innocent. I don't think so. The innocent are innocent and therefore do not need to be protected. I have changed the names in this story so the guilty don't hire lawyers and sue.

I recently realized that I never know when I am assuming. In the moment it happens, assumption simply looks like how reality is. I find out I assumed when the assumption turns into trouble. In the Air Force we used to say something similar to, "Assumption is the mother of screw up!"

My friend and longtime fishing buddy, Ron, told me one day that he wanted to take his brother Mike fishing with us. I don't always recognize a bad idea when I first hear it. Trouble frequently starts out as a fun idea.

I knew that Mike wasn't a rocket surgeon but I "assumed" that he was sane. I agreed that Mike could accompany us on the trip to Lake Cumberland which meanders across the Tennessee/Kentucky line just northeast of Nashville.

Back in those days there was a major disagreement between the Tennessee Wildlife Resources Management and the Kentucky equivalent. I guess that government employees love to controvert. It protects their jobs by showing that they are doing something.

It's a bit fuzzy now but as I recall the hassle had to do with creel limits, or maybe size limits, on bass. What isn't fuzzy is that if you didn't have a Kentucky license, you'd better make damned sure you stayed on the Tennessee side of the state line which roughly bisected the lake.

Horror stories about fanged Kentucky Game Wardens with evil intentions abounded among anglers in all of the tackle shops, bait stores, pool rooms and other liar's hangouts in our area.

That Saturday morning broke clear and cool. A cold front had passed through during the night so I figured we were in for a tough day of fishing. I've never understood why fish don't want to eat after a cold front passes. It always makes me want to order pizza.

We launched the boat around 7 AM and by midday we'd had zero bites and we'd tried every lure out of what I had always referred to as "Ron's Jolly Green Giant Memorial Tackle Box". Ron was one of those fishermen who had to have every lure made and he had to have them all with him every trip. I had asked him as we loaded the boat that morning, "You don't think that tackle box is too heavy for the boat, do you? I'd hate to sink out there. Maybe you should put some wheels on it so you don't hurt your back." I guess his sense of humor was on back order as he had just glowered at me in response.

The mammoth tackle box had a top latch that when released would allow you to raise four hinged trays on either side to expose ample storage room in the

13

bottom. Ron had the habit of throwing just used lures into the bottom of the box to be sorted and organized later but apparently later had not come around in quite a while. The bottom of the box looked like a closeout table at a tackle shop that had just taken a direct hit.

We'd tried every trick we knew that morning except the unbeatable Dupont Spinner. In case you're not from the South and are therefore unfamiliar with the Dupont Spinner; it is a rock tied to a stick of dynamite, made by Dupont, and the fish spin as they come up after it goes off. We had tried everything else.

Noonish we decided to stop at a small cove on an island roughly in the middle of the lake and eat lunch. Seemed innocent enough...how much trouble can we get into eating lunch? Stay tuned.

We beached the boat and were dining under a big oak on gourmet peanut butter and jelly sandwiches when a Fox Squirrel (Rodentia Sciuridae) wandered out on a limb directly above Mike's head. The Fox Squirrel is native to our part of the country and is distinguished from his smaller cousins by his darker coat, tan face and enormous size (by squirrel standards).

Mike reached inside his coat and pulled out a previously concealed pistol and before we could yell, "**STOP!**" He took dead aim and shot the squirrel.

It tumbled out of the tree and landed at Mike's feet. As he picked it up he said, "I told my wife I was bringing dinner home and we obviously aren't going to catch any fish today…what are you guys doing?"

"We're getting the Hell outta here!" Ron said as he and I quickly picked up the picnic supplies and headed for the boat.

Mike grabbed the squirrel and followed us grumbling, "No big deal, guys. What's your hurry?"

About then we heard the unmistakable sound of high speed propellers. Ron turned to me as we sat down in the boat, "Game Warden! Are we on the Tennessee side?"

"I don't know, pretty close I think but it won't matter. This lake is state park on both sides and we aren't even supposed to have a gun, much less hunt."

Mike popped open Ron's Jolly Green Giant Memorial Tackle Box, lifted the trays, tossed the squirrel into the bottom and snapped it shut.

The Kentucky Game Wardens had a really neat boat. It was a center console with twin 150's and it pulled up right next to us as we pushed off. "What'd you boys shoot?" asked the uglier of the two uniformed knuckle-draggers. Those guys were clearly spending too much time in the weight room.

Ron said later, "Looked to me like between them they could have bench pressed Delaware."

Ron spoke up. "We didn't shoot anything. We heard a shot from over thataway." he said, pointing in the opposite direction from which our tormenters had arrived.

I was puckered up tight. If these guys even asked for our licenses the rest of the day was going to be rough as a stucco toilet seat. "Sounded like a pistol to me." I added, looking in the direction Ron had indicated.

The tackle box jumped with a thump. My heart stopped and my life flashed before my eyes. We were dead meat!

Ron maintained his cool. He had been married a long time and was used to thinking fast when in trouble. He casually put his foot up on the top of the box to prevent further thumping.

"You boys sure you didn't shoot?" asked Godzilla again.

By this time Mike had his English back, "No, sir. We're not even armed 'cause we thought we were in a state park." Mike had always believed that if you're going to tell a lie you may as well be thorough.

I assume my Guardian Angel made a big bonus that day because the wind direction was perfect for us. I could still smell the cordite from Mike's gun but they apparently couldn't. "You boys have you a nice day." said Godzilla as they fired up the 150's and pulled out of the cove. We still don't know if Godzilla's partner spoke passable English.

We didn't start the engine. We just sat there, drifting in the cove about 20 feet off of the beach and tried to learn to breathe again.

There is a sort of a hangover that accompanies an adrenaline overdose. My legs were weak and my hands were shaking and angry doesn't quite cover what I was feeling in my guts. When I could talk again I made a very imaginative suggestion to Mike about where he should store that pistol.

I think he was about to respond with something creative about my lineage when the tackle box began to jump around again. Ron had taken his foot off of it as the wardens' boat had disappeared. He reached down, released the catch and lifted out the trays.

That Fox Squirrel came flying up out of that box like the space shuttle blasting off for orbit. He cleared the side of the boat on the fly and he was a total mess. He had lures stuck all over him and some of them were stuck to each other and trailed behind him like a bride's train. And do you know that was the luckiest squirrel I ever heard tell of. He caught 4 bass before he got to the bank!

(I warned you that you'd believe some of the lies! I thought I'd better tell you this was a lie because my friend, Will believed it when he read the rough draft and he was worried about the squirrel.)

Cousin John

My friend Darin Jay Morrissey is a fine fisherman.
He is six feet two inches of love and laughter and I
like him so much that I insult him every time I get a
chance.

He and I like to fish together from my fifteen year old
pontoon on the lakes in middle Tennessee. The
pontoon is more like a floating den than a boat. It has
sofas, easy chairs and a radio with a cassette tape
player…I already told you it was fifteen years old.
The forty horse four stroke pushes her along at a
stately ten knots… we think…the speedometer died
quietly and alone sometime during the winter of '96.

Darin Jay, his mother always referred to him that way
so it's good enough for me, called me one day to
announce that his cousin from New Jersey was
coming to town for a week and wanted to fish with
us.

"New Jersey?" I asked, "Is his passport in order? Has
he had all of his shots?"

Darin didn't swear much as a rule but he made
exceptions for me occasionally, "Dammit, don't be
that way. We gotta be nice to him. He's Momma's
sister's boy and he's been living in a suburb of New
York City all his life. Aunt Sarah thinks he needs
some time away from what they call "The City".

I had him going and couldn't resist, "If you bring him on my boat I'm probably gonna lie to him. You know that."

"I wouldn't bring the Pope on your boat and expect you not to lie to him."

I thought that was uncalled for but Darin was clearly suffering over this cousin's impending trip so I just let it pass.

A few days later I was in the water scraping the bottom of one of the pontoons when Darin and Cousin John arrived. I climbed the ladder and stuck out my hand. As we shook, Cousin John made a noise that sounded like he was trying to speak. "What did you say?"

He made the noise again. I leaned over to Darin Jay and whispered, "The lad has a speech impediment."

"No, he doesn't. He's just got such a bad case of Yankee that he almost can't talk at all."

"Oh, that explains it. I'll try to listen more closely."

I'll give Cousin John credit. He smiled. I suspect that Darin Jay had warned him about me.

I fired up the engine and headed out to deeper water.

Cousin John caught several white and black speckled fish and referred to them as "Crappie". No tellin' what an uneducated Yankee might say.

Being from New Jersey I doubted that he would understand but I tried to help him with his English as much as time permitted.

"Cousin John, this may be difficult for you but there are certain things that no self respectin' Tennessee boy will put in his mouth. 'Croppie' is the correct pronunciation of that fish's name."

He never did get it.

We were fishing over some deep cover a while later when I heard a sound that frequently accompanied our boy Darin Jay. He and Cousin John had lunched on hot dogs and baked beans prior to arriving at my boat, if you are wondering what the sound was.

Darin said, "Did you hear that? That was one of those Tennessee Barking Spiders. I'm sure glad they aren't dangerous because that sounded like a big one."

Cousin John found his way into my heart with his response. "That may or may not have been a Tennessee Barking Spider but I can tell you for sure; whatever it was it sure as Hell has one serious case of bad breath."

Free Range Fishing

I've mentioned my friend Ron a number of times in my stories and I assume he is still my friend after I've told so many tales about him. This is a most unusual story as Ron doesn't look too bad in it.

Our neighborhood coffee shop is a hangout for a number of guys and gals who should be at work. We gather there to drink good coffee and tell bad stories. Ron, who has been my accomplice on a number of these undertakings, says that our mission is for the crowd to doubt our true stories and believe the lies. We bat close to a thousand.

One day a few months ago, Ron was telling us about a trip out West he was about to embark on. Arizona, I think he said. Then he added, "They say it's a dry heat, they say but that's what the sign over Hell's front door says, too."

I suggested that he was going to go into fishing withdrawal if he stayed over two weeks. He had been hospitalized for it for a short period during the preceding winter and was just off of the medication.

He said he was working on a book about the old West and had to do some research. He estimated he'd be gone at least a month. "Not to worry," he said. "One of the Arizona natives is going to take me chicken fishing."

One of our victims hit the bait, "Chicken fishing? I don't believe it."

Ron picked up the slack, "I didn't either until he showed me some pictures. The Free Range Western Chicken is a delicacy. They were almost hunted to extinction a decade ago but the wildlife guys were able to get the Arizona State Legislature to stop all hunting on that species for a couple of years and now you can only fish for them."

I adjusted the drag, "Chickens have awfully small mouths. How do you catch 'em?"

Ron's face lit up. "Well, at least someone here has the good sense to realize he doesn't know everything about everything. They use trout hooks and four pound mono. They fish from cover, kind of like a duck blind and they have to go out before first light to catch 'em when they're feeding." Ron believed that an intricate lie was always easier to sell to his prey than a simple one.

"They don't get too big for the four pound line if you've set your drag right. The Western Free Range Chickens rarely go over three pounds but, I'm told they put up a good fight and are great to eat."

None of his victims was really hooked yet but several were tasting the bait.

When he returned a couple of weeks later his wife was the one who actually set the hook and reeled everyone in. A local grocery store had recently added a deli and was selling baked, spiced whole chickens. One afternoon she bought two and brought them to the coffee shop as Ron was regaling his targets with additional details about his desert chicken-fishing trip.

Doubt still loomed large on the faces of all of Ron's victims until...

"Sorry I'm late," his bride said as she served hunks of chicken to the assembled doubters. "Took a bit longer to cook than regular chickens. I guess they're a bit tougher 'cause of being Free Range and they taste a bit gamey, don't you think?"

They say that some people are just born with a natural ability to sell anything to anyone. If she ever gets a job selling Rolls Royce's, I suspect we're all going to be riding around in style...broke.

Her First Fish

There is a fish native to this part of the world that most people around here call Rock Bass, Black Perch or Goggle Eye. I don't guess I've ever seen one much over two pounds. It's basically green like the largemouth and features black tips on all of its fins but its most prominent feature is a pair of bright red eyes.

I've been calling them Party Bass since an old friend of mine noted that back in his heavy drinking days his eyes used to look just like that fish's every Saturday and Sunday morning.

I'm hoping the name "Party Bass" sticks. I think the fish would approve and, as you probably know, you're very lucky in this life if you get a nickname you like.

I have a very serious case of "Fisherman". I'm told that if I admit this to a reputable psychiatrist he won't take me as a patient. There is apparently no treatment or cure for this chronic ailment.

A few years ago I began to date the most beautiful woman I'd ever seen. Her beauty is not only physical but also spiritual and she has the most unusual perception of reality I've ever come across.

As it became obvious to me that I wanted to spend the rest of my life with her, it only seemed fair for me to take the big risk of warning her of my condition. She deserved to know.

She was undeterred by my malady and suggested that I take her fishing. What a great idea! I would have never thought of it myself as I had been hiding my disorder for many years.

We sat on the curb in front of my apartment a few days later and I taught her to use open-faced spinning tackle. She was a quick study.

The next Saturday we launched a canoe on one of the many small rivers in my beloved Tennessee and began to fish. She was a natural but she insisted on a few changes to our approach. We would only fish with single hook artificials as too many fish swallowed live bait. Plus we would pinch all barbs down and we would release everything we caught. To quote her, "We're not mad at the fish and besides, I don't want to eat any fish that I'm personally acquainted with."

First she caught several bluegills and I noticed she appeared to be whispering to each one before dropping it back into the water. I asked her what she was saying to them.

"Oh, I just give them some advice before I release them."

"Advice to fish...like what?" I couldn't wait to find out.

She smiled that sunrise smile of hers and said, "Like, 'don't eat anymore plastic' or 'have a good life or 'you're a great fighter'; or 'nice to meet you,' or 'I really like your river'; that sort of thing."

I hope I don't ever get used to her.

I claim that when she hooked her first smallmouth later that day, she and the fish jumped in unison. She probably wouldn't have landed that smallie without my coaching, "Sit Down! Sit! Sit! Don't Stand! Sit! We're in a Canoe! Sit!" She was very excited.

Several years later we put together a canoe float and fishing party with eight friends. We had been planning the trip for a long time or we would probably have canceled as there had been a lot of rain and the river was muddy and high.

I told my buddies as we unloaded, "Don't bring your fishing tackle, just canoe today. These conditions are poor and we won't catch much anyway. Besides, my bride is going to out fish all of us by a ton."

I was just trying to help.

They guffawed, "No way does she out fish any one of us! No way!"

My Uncle Frank used to say, "Some people are just naturally hard to help." He was right that day. There were only twelve fish captured that day. I got two. She got eight.

I eventually got used to the idea that on almost every trip she was going to catch more and bigger fish than

I was. Not a problem for me because I get to go fishing and I get to spend the day with her. For me fishing isn't a competitive sport. It's a team sport. I guess having her in my life has helped lessen my case of testosterone poisoning so competing isn't as important as it used to be.

One day not too long after her first fishing trip we went to a park which has a small stream. I caught my biggest Party Bass ever that day. This elegant lady stood there cheering, wearing an old pair of jeans and a surplus fatigue shirt. I'm not sure when I actually fell in love with her but that was the first day I was sure I would love her forever.

Hey, Big Ole Fish

Uncle Willie was a character but that seems to be all we have in my family. I well remember the day his son, my older cousin Don, and I put a car bomb on Willie's '58 Chevy and then came up with an excuse for Willie to take us somewhere.

As we walked to the car I was afraid Don was going to give the gag away as he was giggling. Don got in the back seat and I mounted shotgun as Uncle Willie turned the key. **BANG!** And smoke billowed from under the hood.

Willie grabbed his chest, laid his head over on his shoulder and cried, "My Heart! My Heart! Get a doctor!"

I raced out of the car like I'd been shot out of a cannon and was halfway to the house when I heard the laughter behind me. It turns out that Don had experienced a rare moment of sanity after we had wired the car. During that rare moment he had realized that telling his father so they could turn the joke onto me was a smart move, as he had high hopes of driving that same car on a date that very night.

What I thought I had learned that day was not to trust my relatives…bad idea. A few days later Uncle Willie brought home a yellow-meated watermelon. I'd never heard of such a thing and, being eleven years old, was sure I already knew everything there was to know about everything. Therefore this alleged watermelon was really a vegetable closely akin to a squash which I had already established through personal experience, tasted horrible, so I declined to even try it.

Willie and the rest of the family dug in and finished the melon off in short order, so he went out and bought another one. I continued to resist everyone's suggestions that I at least try it as I was certain I wouldn't like it because I still believed everything I thought.

It was much later that summer when I finally tried a piece when no one else was looking. It was wonderful! I am still trying to learn to stop believing what I think if I haven't really tried whatever it is.

A few days later my father and Uncle Willie charted a boat in Galveston, Texas and took me and Don out for a day of fishing for Gaff-top Catfish. The Gaff-top is a saltwater bottom fish that typically runs from three to five pounds and fries up real tasty.

We anchored a few minutes after launch and Willie and my father began to catch fish. Don and I weren't even getting bites. Being young men we were a bit energetic and continuously wound in our hooks in to check the bait. I realize now that a catfish would have had to be in superb physical condition to catch up with our hooks.

I studied Willie and noticed that occasionally he would bend his head down near his reel and shortly afterward he would hook a fish. Sneaking up closer I was able to discern that he was whispering to his reel but I couldn't make out what he was saying.

I finally asked him and he replied, "I'm talking down the line to the fish. It works kinda like a phone line."

I was certain he was pulling my chain but as I watched he continued to whisper to his reel and to catch fish while I sustained zero hits. After about an hour of studying this phenomenon, I asked him, "What do you say to them?"

He leaned over his reel, "Hey, a big ole fish, get on this line!" And he immediately hooked another one...and me.

At his instruction I sat really still for about five minutes and then whispered, "Hey, a big ole fish, get on this line." And a few moments later I caught my first fish of the day. I spent the rest of the day talking down the line to the fish.

Today I am convinced that catfish feed by following the scent of the bait and that a still bait will catch the most catfish but occasionally, when they aren't biting, I look around to make sure no one else is watching and whisper to my reel, "Hey, a big ole fish, get on this line."

Rest in peace, Uncle Willie, and thanks for teaching me how to talk down the line.

SMALLMOUTH BASS

My friend Ron is a very good smallmouth bass fisherman. He is exceptionally good. In fact he is almost as good as I am. I'm sure he'll be proud I said that about him when he reads this.

He has several unusual techniques I'd like to share with other smallmouth lovers. I think he has watched too many fishing shows on TV. When we float the rivers of our beloved Tennessee he is constantly throwing his lure into trees. He says some famous tournament fishermen say to fish in the trees. I'll admit that I've heard that myself, but I'm almost certain it is the submerged trees in impoundments like the TVA lakes; not the ones innocently growing on the bank that he usually targets.

Sometimes when he throws into a tree or bush that is overhanging the water, if the lure doesn't lodge in the branches, he opens the bale and lowers the bait all the way down to the water. Then he jiggles it on the surface for a few minutes. I've seen him catch a lot of fish that way. He always says he threw it there on purpose but I rarely believe him.

The worst part is that he always seems to get the lures out of the trees. I'd swear that I get hung up on the bottom more often than he gets hung up fishing in those trees.

I take it all back. The worst part was that he and I canoed and fished together for many years with me in the back of the canoe all the time. In case you don't know, the guy in the front paddles 1% of the time and fishes 99% while the guy in the back drives the canoe 40% of the time and fishes about 60%.

Every time he tried the back we were all over the river and we nearly turned over several times with him driving.

One day I happened to go out to his back yard where I spotted a well-worn canoe, cleverly concealed under a tarp. That #!@&*% owned a canoe himself and had been faking that he couldn't steer a canoe for over ten years so he could do most of the fishing! That's why he is the butt of so many of these stories.

He once caught a smallmouth without even having a lure in the water. He and I each had a lady in the front of our canoes out on the Buffaloe River. We had selected a particular sandbar where we'd decided to take out for a rest and a picnic. As we approached the sandbar Ron reeled his lure up to about two feet from the end of his rod and placed the butt end of the rod on the bottom of the canoe with the tip hanging over the side which left his lure hanging about a foot above the water. A half pound smallie came flying up out of the water and grabbed Ron's lure and hooked itself. Ron grabbed his rod just before that bass took it out of his canoe.

If I hadn't seen it myself, I'd probably be doubting it like you are now.

Ron is with the police force in our town and has spent many years with the K-9 unit. They have several dogs they call "cadaver dogs". Unfortunately there are a number of drownings every year in the lakes around our town. When one occurs, if the body doesn't surface, they put one of these dogs in the bow of a boat and slowly cruise the lake until the dog comes on point. The divers go down where the dog pointed and always recover the body.

Ron called me one day and said he had a friend in Kentucky who said he had a dog that would point smallmouth bass. It was in the blood lines of the cadaver dogs.

I didn't believe it but, like most serious smallie fishermen, I'll try absolutely anything if it has a chance to catch more bass. One Saturday we drove up to Scottsville to the home of this dog breeder that Ron was so excited about.

The dog was as ugly as a rear view mirror full of flashing blue lights. The breeder said he had named him Rusty, not after his coat which was mostly black with some brown spots, but after an old sobered up alcoholic friend of his who, at the bottom of his drinking career, had wet his pants so many times that his zipper rusted shut.

Apparently the dog was a frequent user of the potty.

The breeder took us out on Lake Cumberland for an afternoon of fishing with this forty-pound mongrel guide. Whenever the dog came on point we fished. I was amazed at how many smallies we caught that day.

Several dollars later we headed back to Nashville with Rusty, our new secret weapon.

A few days later we were out on Center Hill Lake about an hour east of Nashville and Rusty was in excellent form. He said the smallies were on a flat near the dam and he was right. We caught several really big ones and then they stopped biting so we decided to cross to a similar flat on the other side of the deep water just about a quarter of a mile from the dam.

As I pulled up the trolling motor and Ron started the engine a big catfish surfaced right in front of Rusty and snarled. Rusty chased that catfish down into a hundred feet of water and that was the last time we ever saw him.

The breeder has been unable to train any more dogs like Rusty so we are stuck fishing without a qualified guide. We still fish for smallmouth but we're always a bit sad that Rusty isn't with us. In his honor, we usually take a few moments to pee in the lake. I'm sure Rusty would like that.

(You have to admit that I'm a really gifted liar! Will believed this one, too.)

Catfish Humor

I was recently on my old pontoon boat with my two so-called friends, Darin Jay and Will for a Sunday afternoon cruise. A day of fishing, teasing each other mercilessly and tall tales promised to be both fun and intellectually stimulating. It doesn't take much to stimulate the intellect of two digit IQ's like my shipmates were sporting that day.

We are at a change of the seasons and the fish are a bit more unpredictable than usual. Working hard on several favorite honey holes had produced one good smallmouth (any smallmouth is a good one) and a few small Crappie (pronounced Croppie in case any novices are reading this) in two hours. Not a good start.

Darin Jay suggested we try some deeper water which produced nothing at all, which is what usually happens when we try his suggestions. I thought we might find some good slab Crappie back in my favorite cove. I, of course, was correct.

Using small lures on light line we soon boated several keepers but we weren't keeping that day. We were just playing so they were released unharmed but I suppose embarrassed to have tried to eat plastic. Crappie are quite self-conscious.

I then skillfully moved the boat up over a submerged roadbed and Will and I began to work it slow and deep while Darin Jay tried to remember how to tie on a lure.

I got a strong hit and was suddenly loosing line as the drag sang for the first time that day. Darin Jay spoke up, "I sure hope that's a Crappie!" he mused. "If it is, we'll probably be on the front page of the paper and maybe even on TeeVee."

A few minutes later I finally pulled an eight pound catfish up to the surface and Will netted it. I know that lots of folks like to eat them, and on occasion I'm one of them but handling a large flopping catfish is not one of my favorite things to do. I'd rather go to the dentist.

I was going to simply remove the hook with my pliers and lower the fish back into the water without ever taking it out of the net. "No," they cried in unison. "We've got to have a picture."

I must have some kind of learning disability as by this age I should know that anything both of them want to do is probably a very bad idea. I pulled the hook and used the pliers to lift the catfish up by the lower jaw. The fish and I struck manly poses and Curley and Moe began to take pictures.

At about photo number four the catfish was suddenly struck with a savage case of dysentery. This particular fish was apparently very well nourished. Darrin Jay later offered that the catfish had most likely been drinking water from a tap in Juarez the night before.

One thing about dysentery, you don't have to wait for it. There are never any back orders. They ship it all at once. Splat! And there is an accompanying aroma to round out the presentation.

That fish pooped all over my right leg and splattered most of the double seat next to the captain's chair, not to mention half of the carpet.

My purported friends had obviously never seen anything that funny in their dreary lives. They were both bent over like they were the ones with gastric distress and Darin Jay laughed so hard that he added sound effects to the proceedings by intermittently passing gas which they also found to be exceptionally amusing.

A few minutes later a red faced Will suggested that I rename my boat the "Poop Deck" and Darin Jay lost control of his exhaust system again as they cackled away.

I suppose if a man had enough close friends, he would have no need at all for enemies. His so-called friends would wear him out without the need of assistance.

Light Chop

I'm told that the Sauger, which is native to Tennessee, is first cousin to the Walleye which is universally acclaimed as one of the best tasting fish that swims in fresh water. From this I deduce that the Sauger is a gourmet treat also. I may never find out.

I tried to find out a few winters ago. Memory says it was a January evening when Ron called. I hadn't heard him this excited since the Redskins won the Super Bowl. "Winter is the best season to catch Sauger and tomorrow will be perfect Sauger fishing weather. The high temperature will be in the early forties and a five to ten knot wind from the South will provide a light chop so the fish can't see us. It's perfect!"

I have a serious, untreatable learning disability known as "fisherman" so I agreed to this insanity. Sometimes I forget what I know and I know that I don't like to be cold and that I'm a better fisherman when I can feel my hands.

We launched the boat around 9 AM. I was pleased to note that at least the Sauger didn't insist that we arrive before dawn. That was the only positive thing that happened that day.

I'm no meteorologist but I'd say that the predicted five to ten knots out of the South was more like to ten to twenty out of the North and the light chop Ron had forecast was white-capping.

Ron had a honey hole selected where the current regularly scooped out a small depression in about 20 feet of water. He said the Sauger loved to lie in that hole and feed during the winter months. I kept wondering where they fed in July but refrained from asking.

Using a new depth finder for guidance, we dropped the anchor just upstream from his secret honey hole and grabbed our rods. By the time I had my lure in casting position we had blown/drifted off of the hole. I pulled up the anchor as Ron started the engine and we ran back upstream and, by the way, up wind and repositioned the boat.

As I dropped the anchor this time Ron said, "I'll run the trolling motor to help the anchor and you fish."

Now we're on a great plan! He works and I fish. As I once again prepared to cast he said, "I've got this *&%*#* trolling motor set on 5 to help the anchor and we're still blowing downstream."

We spent the next hour or so trying to position the boat upstream from the magic fishing spot long enough for me to get a lure all the way to the bottom. We never succeeded.

He finally pointed across the river and offered "Plan B", "Why don't we go up that tributary and try our luck out of some of this wind?"

I would have rather eaten tofu than continue to be outdoors that day but I also suffer from a severe case of testosterone poisoning and was not about to suggest we go home and watch the ballgame by the fire as I knew I would never hear the end of it if I did.

Seemed to me that we never had a high temperature that day...only a low and if we really did have a high in the early forties, it must have been right after midnight.

As he was knocking the ice...yes, ice...off of the first eye of his rod he said, "It's colder than my first wife out here today...perfect Sauger weather. I'm sure we'll catch some."

He has a long history of being sure of things that are actually incorrect.

We fished for eight hours that day and only caught two of the illusive Sauger. We released both of them because they were just slightly smaller than the lures.

Amazing as it may seem to a non-fisherman, the day was a total success. It was the beginning of a long and fruitful friendship between two men who suffer from similar cases of "fishing pox".

Tennessee State Record

My favorite fishing buddy, Ron and I were bellied up to a neighborhood coffee bar, telling lies and working each other over with good natured insults as we loved to do, when the rather well-nourished lady friend of another fishing addict arrived. She ordered what I've come to think of as a "coffee milkshake" along with two of those softball sized muffins and joined us.

"You guys are both fishermen aren't you?"

We pled guilty as charged, Your Honor, and threw ourselves on the mercy of the court.

"Have you ever fished Center Hill Lake?"

"You betcha!" Center Hill is a Tennessee Valley Authority lake about an hour east of Nashville and is one of the most beautiful bodies of water in the world. It's usually very clear and is always fun to fish.

I replied, "Center Hill is such a great fishery that even my buddy Ron here can catch fish in it most of the time."

Before he could respond with a suitable barb for me she continued, "Jerry just got back from there and had a really great guide for the weekend."

It wasn't probable that our definition of a "really great guide" and hers' would match. I've long said that any guide who is having a bad day and says,

"The fish are confused today" isn't much of a man, much less of a guide.

I don't think the fish are EVER confused. They know exactly what they are doing all of the time. It's the guide who is confused and one who won't admit it is off of my list forever. I also think that those who will hire this kind of guide deserve what they get. But back to the coffee shop…

Ron asked her, "What made this guide so great?"

"Well, they caught a lot of fish."

Ron and I agreed that was one characteristic we looked for in a guide.

"He also cleaned them."

OK, more points but we were nowhere near "really great" yet as we didn't know of any guides, great or otherwise who didn't clean the fish.

"And he wrapped them up in two-person meal-sized packages and labeled them."

We approved and allowed as to how that was certainly a good sign.

Then Ron asked the wrong question, "He labeled them? What kind of fish were they?"

"Red Snapper," she said proudly.

I grabbed my stomach and raced into the men's room as Ron bent over at the waist in a severe coughing fit.

It was several minutes later when I felt settled enough to come out of the restroom. Ron's face was still red and he continued to cough intermittently. "Coffee went down the wrong pipe." He said as he pointed at his throat. "Damned stuff is hard to exhale."

I agreed immediately, "Yes, it is and occasionally it gives me a sudden case of the green-apple quick-step."

He helped me with my story, "Yes, I've seen it hit you like that before. Are you ok?"

"Yes, I'm ok but I think I'll head home now."

Ron was on the idea of getting out of there like a duck on a Junebug. He glanced at his watch, "I'm gonna be late if I don't leave right now."

He and I later congratulated each other on the fancy moves we'd hastily concocted to cover our laughter as well as the swift exits but we've both been bothered for a long time about that guide. He wasn't a really great guide at all in my book.

A truly great guide would never have cleaned those fish. He would have had them mounted because they were undoubtedly the Tennessee State Record Red Snappers as Red Snapper is a salt water fish and, in case you didn't know, Tennessee isn't on an ocean.

(I hope she doesn't read this, cause this one's true!)

Yellow Creek

Yellow Creek wanders around Dickson and several other Counties in Middle Tennessee like a lost tourist. It is poorly named as it isn't yellow at all. Being spring fed it flows clear as well water.

I was first introduced to it in the summer of 1987 by my friend Ron. He said he had an uncle who owned several hundred acres of farm land that included a few hundred yards of the stream. We parked in the farmhouse's driveway which lent credence to Ron's story that his uncle actually owned it. As you may know, fishermen are occasionally known to stretch the truth a bit if necessary.

We "wet waded" which is to say we wore sandals and shorts and had tackle boxes that slung over our shoulders or attached to our bodies like baby Koalas. I'd guess we splashed two miles that day and caught one hundred and twenty fish after we started counting. Twelve species was the final tally, mostly small, all fun.

I had become a catch and release guy the winter before by accident. In the summer of 1986 I'd caught a 5+ pound largemouth and was too tired to clean it when I got home. I'd been told that you could freeze a fish whole and then clean it when you were ready to cook it. Many months later I found it under some steaks, freezer burned and inedible. I'd had to throw it away. That broke my heart and I vowed never to let that happen again.

We had several unforgettable trips on Yellow Creek but I suppose the most memorable was with his son Lance a few weeks before his United States Army Division deployed to Iraq. We didn't catch as many fish as usual that day and I've always thought it was because we were a bit more like a circus parade than a fishing expedition. Cajoling each other and teasing about various things is not conducive to catching a lot of fish.

Late in the day we happened onto a good sized pool and, for a change, worked it quietly to good success. Looking further upstream, I noticed at the top of the pool, what we always called an ambush point. It's a place where a bass can lay in a relatively calm piece of water like an eddy and patrol a large amount of faster moving water, darting out to capture various unfortunate creatures as the current carries them by.

I skillfully, as usual, put my lure just upstream from the ambush point and allowed the current to pick it up. A smallmouth bass about two pounds hit it like a train and immediately went berserk jumping and racing all over the pool. The best part was that Ron and Lance were both knee deep in the pool and had to hop over my line several times like a couple of schoolgirls playing jump rope. I almost lost the fish because I was laughing so hard at them.

Ron and I both treasure the memories of that day and when it is just the two of us, we like to tell the story to each other. I write this in memorial to Lance as that was his last fishing trip.

OTHER LIES

Add On's

Many years have passed since the events reported here occurred and the chain of stores in question no longer exists. Due to these facts I suggested to my lawyer that it was probably ok for me to use the actual names of the individuals and of the chain in this story. My lawyer suggested that if I did so, I should retain another lawyer as he was resigning and that I should see a good psychiatrist. Therefore I have changed or deleted the actual names.

The Annual National Sales Meeting and Awards Banquet was held in the Crystal Ballroom of the Palmer House in Chicago. It was a dressy affair and a one hour open bar had created the desired effect of lubricating the proceedings.

Seated up on the dais with the Vice President of Sporting Goods Sales, the National Sales Manager and all six Regional Sales Managers was a visibly uncomfortable Darin Jay Morrissey, a country boy from the outskirts of Nashville, Tennessee. The fine steak dinner and several drinks had not swayed Darin from his decision to fire his guardian angel for negligence. A good guardian angel would have provided him with a heart attack or other plausible excuse for missing the event.

As the dessert dishes were being cleared the Vice President called the meeting to order. "Ladies and Gentlemen, as you know the whole chain has had a banner year and Sporting Goods led all departments in gross sales increase and in profit dollars."

A standing ovation allowed several of the less motivated celebrants to exit, undetected. Darin Jay was not one of the lucky escapees.

The VP continued, "We are here to celebrate the whole department for sure but also to honor one of our own. This man made the single largest sporting goods sale ever made to one individual in the history of our company."

The standing O was a good bit less enthusiastic.

"Darin, would you please stand up and tell us the amazing story of your record breaking add-on sale"?

Darin Jay rose to just barely polite applause. Those who had failed to sneak out at the last opportunity settled in for a long harangue.

"Well," said our boy, "I sold this ole boy a fishin' pole and suggested that the new Shimmano 500 was the perfect reel to match the rod so he bought that, too. I asked what kind of line he used and he said he didn't have any line so I offered to load it with 10 pound mono at no charge. He seemed to be pretty pleased about the free line so, while I was putting it on his reel, I asked him to look at our new "Assortment A" of fresh water lures and he bought that, too."

Darin paused, which gave most of his audience the false hope that he was finished but he was only getting a drink of water.

He continued, "I said, 'you know if you try to carry those lures in your jeans pocket those treble hooks will cut your legs to shreds and besides, the one you want will always be on the bottom.' He bought the new Big Box tackle box with the slide out drawers on the end and the lift out trays."

"He seemed happy with that so I decided to go big, 'How many really good fishermen do you know who don't have a boat?'"

"None, I guess."

"Right you are. How do you like that little twenty four footer over there?"

Darin was warming up to his story and the crowd was now frozen like a museum full of statues. "That's a really nice looking boat." he said, "does the trailer come with it?"

"'Sure does,' I said and then I smacked him with, 'How fast do you think you can paddle that boat with your hands?'"

The laughter was deafening and turned into applause that went on long enough for Darin to have a couple more sips of his water.

"He bought the new Mercury two twenty-five and a five horse trolling motor and deluxe battery."

"Next I said one word to him, 'Fishfinder,' and that was all it took. He got the new Color Side-View Fish and Depth Finder with all of the bells and whistles."

"I was about to tally up the sale when I noticed his wedding ring so I said, 'You're a married man, aren't you?'"

"He said, 'Yes, I am,' so I said, 'I'd bet your wife would like to learn to water ski.'"

"He bought two sets of regular skis, two slalom skis, two ski ropes, a book on water skiing, four life vests, and a fire extinguisher."

Darin sat down to a thunderous ovation that lasted over five minutes.

As the applause finally died down the Vice President stood back up, "Darin, that's truly the best example of an add-on sale I've encountered in my thirty years in the business."

More applause was followed by the VP's last remark, "Our latest market research analysis has shown us that we lose over fifty percent of our customers on the approach, the open. How did you hit this guy?"

Darin stood up, rather sheepishly looking at his shoes, "Well, sir it was a Friday afternoon around 3:30 when this ole boy come up to me and said kinda quiet like, 'Hey, Buddy, do you know where I can buy some tampons?' So I said to him, 'Listen here

Fella, you ain't doin' nothin' this weekend, why don't you go fishin'?'"

(Gotcha again!)

Uncle Frank

My Uncle Frank was a gambler, pool player, golfer, beer drinker, ladies' man, fisherman and all around nare-do-well; and of course, my hero. On one of his sojourns with us he offered to take me bluegill fishing. My mother asked him, "How long will you be gone?"

"It depends on the fish." He replied. "If they aren't biting very well we'll probably stay all day and fish as hard as we can. If they're biting about average we'll stay all day as this is what we expect. If they're biting great we'll stay all day because you don't get many days like that so, as you can see, it's really up to the fish."

My mother shook her head and I laughed. I laughed because I didn't understand that he was actually telling her the truth.

I hope every boy in America has an Uncle Frank to guide him through the early teen years when he can't hear his idiot parents. Mine was quite a philosopher or at least so appeared to my thirteen-year old eyes and he taught me life lessons that weren't going to be covered in my high school curriculum.

He educated me on the ways of the world; like how to stroke the cue ball instead of hitting it so I could put maximum English on it; how to whittle and sharpen a pocket knife; and how to make instant friends with a dog by scratching him right on the point of his breastbone where he can't scratch

60

himself. He tried to slow down my backswing but was not successful in that endeavor. Mostly, he taught me lessons about life.

"The school yard bully only understands one thing, his own bloody nose. Don't fight if you can get out of it and save face. If you have to fight, throw the first punch. Most fights are one punch long."

"Always put the toilet seat down, even in the men's room. The difference between a good habit and a bad habit is that good habits are easy to break. Putting the seat down is easy to do and the first time she falls in at 3 AM you are going to be weeks convincing her that you really do love her.

"Put the seat down even if you live alone. You plan to have another lady someday so you may as well get it right in the meantime."

Frank cooked the best spaghetti I'd ever eaten one evening so I asked for the recipe. He wrote it out on a piece of paper and folded it up for me. I put it in my jeans pocket and forgot about it. When I opened it several days later, I was reminded how well he knew me. It began:

1. Wash your hands!

"Knowledge is a terrible thing. Once you have it, you can't put it back. You're stuck with it so be very careful of the questions you ask or you'll end up knowing a bunch of stuff you wish you didn't."

"When it hits the fan, the fan never spreads it evenly. Sometimes you'll be right in the line of fire and not even get a whiff. Other times you'll be down the hall with the door closed and innocent and the fan will smear it all over you but in the long run you'll come out ahead if you keep your wits about you."

"When you're busted, come completely clean. If you hold out on the smallest detail of whatever you're guilty of, they will eventually find out. When they do, you will be forever rebuilding their trust. When you're caught, dump the whole bucket."

When you're late for something, you've made a very strong statement as to how valuable you consider the other person's time to be.

"Understand the rules as thoroughly as possible so you can break them effectively and get away with it."

"There are three excellent theories on how to handle women. None of them work."

"Your spiritual assignment will change. When, not if, it does, embrace the new one as quickly as possible and you'll come to love the new one as much as you did the old one."

"If you ain't happy with what you've got, you ain't gonna be happy with what you get. Happiness is an inside job."

"Never bet the other man's game! Never! One of these days the stranger on the next bar stool is going to offer to bet you an amount of money equal to however much you have in your wallet that he can make the Jack of Diamonds jump out of your shirt pocket and piss in your ear. If you bet him you will end up broke with an ear full of piss! Never bet the other man's game!"

This particular piece of wisdom saved my bankroll on numerous occasions. One particular night the fellow on the next stool said, "Let's gamble for a drink."

I agreed and he proposed that we each write the names of 5 of the States on a bar napkin. We'd then exchange napkins and write the capitals. Fortunately I remembered Uncle Frank's warning.

"You can't lose," I said to him, "you know them all perfectly."

He grinned, "Not only that, there are over 150 countries in the world and I know all of their capitals...and can spell them all correctly."

I smiled at him, "I'd guess you've made a pretty penny on that hustle."

"Oh yes, you'd be amazed how many guys will bet big on that one."

Frank said there were only three things I needed to do to make good money shooting pool.

63

"First, get down low so you cab sight down the stick and make sure the stick is running right under your chin.

"Second, don't let anything move except your right wrist. Especially don't let your head or butt come up or change your grip at impact.

"Third, don't ever play anyone who can beat you.

"Do those three things and you can make good money shooting pool."

"Here's how to pack smart for any trip. Spend a few minutes figuring out where all you're going, what kinds of events you'll attend and what sorts of attractions you'll be seeing. With that all in mind, figure out what clothes you'll need and how much money it will all cost. Then, here's the trick, take half as many clothes as you figured and twice as much money. It'll work out just about perfect every time."

Wife

My wife has some of the most unusual ideas I've ever come across.

We were changing the clocks to Daylight Savings Time one evening when she said, "These politicians! If they're going to mess with the time, why don't they get it right?"

I've been in the outfit long enough to know that I want to hear any suggestions she may have about anything. "What would you suggest that they do to get it right?"

She thought for a few moments, "Why don't they make it dark out from like 1 in the afternoon until 3 and we can all take a nap? Then they could give us an extra hour of daylight in the morning AND in the evening."

I'm prepared to vote for that, aren't you?

Another time I heard her apologizing on the phone, "I'm so sorry. I must have dialed the wrong number. Can you tell me did I dial...?" and she gave a number.

She paused for a few moments, listening and then said "I apologize for troubling you. I hope you have a nice day and thanks for being so pleasant."

She turned to me and said, "I think if you dial a wrong number and only miss by only one digit, you should at least get someone you know."

I think so, too.

She knows the names of most of the local wildflowers. I suspect the wildflowers know her name, too. She collects heart-shaped rocks. We find them on the gravel bars as we fish the rivers of Tennessee. You can find them, too. All you have to do is look.

Sometimes she mixes her words up. I like it when she does.

A few years ago I was sitting in front of the TV on Sunday afternoon, watching the U S Open Golf Tournament's last round. My wife was sitting there, too but she was uninterested in the golf. She was spending time with her husband.

I usually watch sports on TV with the sound off as few sportscasters have added to my enjoyment since Tom Brookshire was fired for telling the truth.

One of the Japanese players, I don't remember which one, was in contention on the back nine and we were seeing quite a few of his shots. He was making a charge and had a real chance to win.

On the number 16 Tee he hit a shot that looked a lot like one of mine which is to say it was really bad. That shot undoubtedly cost him his chance to win a major tournament and he knew it immediately. The camera came in close on his face and you could see that he was in anguish.

My wife's compassion overflowed, "Oh, I hope he doesn't commit karaoke!"

I hope so, too. I've been there when people committed karaoke and it is a heinous crime not to mention that there is apparently not a time limit on it.

Charity

Some friends and I meet frequently at a neighborhood coffee shop. It is much like a "home bar" without the alcohol. We solve the world's problems and ruminate on the great philosophical questions like, "If God is all powerful, can He create a rock so large that He can't move it?"

We've actually answered that one and I'll tell you the answer later if I remember. Of all of the things I have left, my forgetter seems to work the best.

A particular pair of the regulars at our coffee klatch are very good friends and among the many things they have in common is the fact that both have been married and divorced **several** times in the last few years. I'd like to observe that one is one, two is a couple and several **is** more than two.

These two frequently and most good naturedly work each other over on the boy/girl thingy. "Are you married again yet?" is a common greeting.

One of them favors ladies who are many years his junior. He was describing a recently found new love when his friend interrupted, "I understand you met her by stopping to help her when her vehicle broke down. As I recall she had a flat on her big-wheel."

The constant exchange of barbs between these two keeps the rest of us in laughter most days.

I had noticed a few months ago that one of this odd pair seemed to be losing weight so I pointed at his midsection and asked, "Are you trying to get down to your fighting weight?"

He grinned, "When I turned forty I decided to stop fighting all together so I no longer have a fighting weight. I'm trying to get down to my dating weight."

One afternoon another of the regulars at the afore mentioned establishment and I were working on what I believe is the single most difficult question any of us ever face: "What do you want?"

Not, "What do you want given that (fill in the blank)", but, "What do you really want for your life?"

We had been feeling our way deeper and deeper into the metaphysical meanings of life, reality and caffeine when one of the odd couple chimed in, "What I really want is to be a philanthropist and sit on the beach writing checks to charity."

His friend immediately responded, "Is Charity one of your X-wives?"

It's not always easy to have deep conversations with these two around.

By the way, the answer to the God's omnipotence question posed above is, "If that's what He wants to do, it's ok with me. Now, what would He have me do next?"

Country Club

I have never been a member of a country club as the love of golf seems to me to be the only reason for joining one and I don't suffer from that particular disorder.

One morning last summer I entered our neighborhood coffee shop a bit later than usual and was met at the door by my so-called friend, Ron. He seemed quite upset. "What's the matter?" I queried in my usual selfless manner.

"It's Joe, not me. He's over there," he said, pointing to a table on the far side by the window.

I should have smelled a rat. These two had set me up before. The most recent time was when Joe had said Ron got locked up on his trip to Milwaukee. I bit hard on that one as Ron is a retired police sergeant. I went right over to him and said, "You went and got yourself arrested on your trip to Wisconsin?"

"No," he responded with that grin I only see when he nails me, "I got locked up. Think I must have eaten too much of their cheese."

Like I said, I should have suspected foul play.

With the hook firmly embedded in my upper jaw I was propelled across the room toward Joe by my terminal need to help a friend in need. His facial expression clearly indicated that he had just run over his own dog, or something else of that magnitude. He was a hurtin' unit for sure. "What happened, Joe?" I asked.

He adjusted the drag as he reeled me in, by looking down, shaking his head and not responding.

I have been the self-appointed chaplain of the outfit for a very long time so I pulled up a chair and just sat with him for a few minutes. Finally I said, "Joe, come on. I'm your friend and you're obviously going to have to talk about whatever this is, sooner or later. Please talk to me."

He looked up at me over his glasses. His pain must have been acute based on his expression. "They've thrown me out of the country club," he said and then buried his face in his hands.

I couldn't believe it. "You were a founding member of that club thirty years ago. Without your energy and know how, not to mention your political savvy, that place would still be a swamp."

He continued to hang his head, "I know it but they're throwing me out."

"Don't you have a two digit membership number? Weren't you the second chairman of the board? Don't you chair the membership committee today?"

"All true," he said as he continued to study his shoes, "but they're throwing me out anyway."

I can't believe it, "Why are they throwing you out?"

"They got me for peeing in the pool."

I was incensed, "Peeing in the pool! Lots of people pee in the pool."

"Not from the high board they don't."

The Drop-Down Answers

Silence may be golden but there are times when every answer I can give is going to get me in trouble and yet silence isn't an option. These are the times when taking the Fifth Amendment won't work. The Drop-Down Answers are the key to surviving these harrowing situations.

Here is a typical example:

My boss has just made a ridiculous statement or a stupid proposal. He has a natural flair and excels in both of these categories. He probably doesn't actually want my opinion; even if he's just asked for it!

It may be that he just wants to hear his own voice. He may just want to feel important by talking without anyone else talking or by talking without anyone else having an opinion or disagreeing. Whichever of these is the case, I'm trapped and I must respond. Silence is not an option and all possible true answers are hazardous to my ability to continue to work here. What to do?

The Drop-Down Answers that can save the day:

Drop-Down Answer Number 1. "Sounds Great."

This is the most flexible of these answers. Please observe the different ways you can deliver this one: SOUNDS GREAT! Sounds Great! Sounds great. sounds great. sounds great. sounds great.

These can be accompanied for emphasis by body language such as facial expressions and/or head and body movements. This does NOT include rolling your eyes.

This one is most useful when you're pretty sure he won't act on his idiot idea anytime soon but really just wants to have his bosshood validated.

Drop-Down Answer Number 2. "Oh."

This Drop-Down Answer acknowledges information has been received (can be good or bad). Besides, you're completely powerless over this information or you wouldn't be using Drop-Downs.

After you deliver your "Oh." he will probably continue to display his brilliance. Should he ask again for your opinion after you've responded with "Oh." you can consult the list for another response. The "Oh." response is only usable once.

Here's an example from a former wife:

"I just got in an auto accident with your son in the car."

"Oh."

Note the period after the word "Oh." That period (like many others) means **STOP**. Everything you say after the period just gets you into trouble.

If you say "Don't ever do that again" after the period, it will have no impact whatsoever on her driving. When talking to certain people in this example, the additional statement after the period might even make the situation worse.

This one is especially effective in the afore mentioned boss talking situation.

If you say, "Oh." he will immediately realize that you have responded and are therefore listening attentively; but five minutes later he won't know what your response was. He just needed a response to confirm that he had an audience.

Drop-Down Answer Number 3 "That's interesting."

This is one of the safer Drop- Down Answers. It doesn't commit you to agreeing or to disagreeing and it leaves you open to use any other Drop-Down Answer as a fallback position later if he asks again.

Jack Nicholson has a great line in the movie, *As Good as It Gets,* "I'll always give you some version of the truth."

This one is a version of the truth as it is probably true that the boss is interested. It does not mean that you are.

Drop-Down Answer Number 4. "No."
This is the most dangerous of the Drop-Down Answers but sometimes you'll have to take the plunge and use it.

This important response is almost exclusively used with someone who is inviting you to engage in a self-destructive action. Also like #2 above, it is followed by a period meaning **STOP**.

The call for this answer is obvious in many cases like: "Would you like me to fire you?"
"No."

"Would you like to go to jail?"
"No."

"Do you want to shoot yourself in the foot?"
"No."

Be alert for tricky questions like this old favorite fight starter:

"Does this dress make my butt look big?"

Same answer: "No." Again, the period means **STOP**.

Move your Personal Danger Warning System to **RED ALERT** following the use of "No." The person who set you up to have to use it may be just warming up and could easily hit you with a cleverly disguised follow up invitation to commit verbal suicide.

Don't forget the all-important period. Anything you say after the period puts you on a slippery slope and you won't like what you find at the bottom of that slope. Anything you say after "No." will extend a conversation that you don't want to participate in.

The only way to not participate is by not participating at all.

For example you could add after your initial, "No.", "What made you think I'd like to be fired or go to jail?" Or "Why did you think I'd want to shoot myself in the foot?"

Any of these continuations will prolong a discussion about you getting fired, going to jail or getting foot-shot. Since you don't want to be fired, jailed or foot-shot you don't want to talk about them at all. So don't! Stop after, "No."!

For the "Big Butt" question you could, in a moment of unguarded honesty, cleverly add, "But you could stand to lose some weight."

I suppose you might want to try this if you were firmly committed to celibacy for the foreseeable future; but I can't imagine any other reason to extend the conversation.

"No." is a loner. It is like sleeping dogs, better left alone. "No." seldom plays well with others and is best left to a solitary existence.

My Uncle Frank, a professional gambler, once told me, "If you can't win, don't play!" All after "No." is playing a game you can't win. Don't play.

Drop-Down Answer Number 5. "I'd like to think about that."

Once again you haven't committed either way plus you've bought an unspecified amount of time. You don't really want to think about it. You really want to think about anything else, at all!

During this time your boss may come to his senses; realize he's making a mistake; and never bring it up again. If he realizes he is making a mistake you can bet he won't bring it up again!

He may also forget all about it and never bring it up again. His boss may clamp down on this obvious error and take you completely out of ever having to address the issue again.

If he does bring it up again you can tell him you're still thinking about it or; if he presses, you can go with any other Drop-Down Answer.

Time is your friend and Drop-Down Answer 5 is the best way to buy some, cheap!

Why do we need the Drop-Down Answers and where did they come from?

A good friend of mine is a police officer. He once told me that more people talk their way into jail than talk their way out.

Another acquaintance who we'll call Fred is the National Poster Boy for this great truth. He actually holds the Tennessee State Record for saying stupid things to authority figures. He does it in many situations but usually concentrates his efforts on doing it to people who have the complete authority and inclination to have him incarcerated for a period of time from a few hours to a few years.

It seems that there had been a sort of a misunderstanding about whether he could leave the State of Tennessee to go gambling in Las Vegas. While in Las Vegas, Fred was able to exercise his amazing ability to **NOT** keep his mouth shut around authority figures, and consequently found himself the guest of the Clark County Sheriff's Department for a short (by Fred's standards) period of time.

By Fred's own admission he had not been his Parole Officer's favorite customer. Shortly after Fred's triumphant return from Las Vegas he was summoned to his P. O.'s office, as he had missed several mandatory appearances during his sojourn with the Clark County Constabulary. He was seriously concerned that he might well leave his appointment with the P.O. in some sort of government conveyance on the way to a destination not of Fred's own choosing; the Davidson County Jail for example and for quite a while.

What to do?

My friend, Wall Street Dan created the Drop-Down Answers for the occasion. He sat Fred down and coached him on them; and extracted from Fred a solemn oath that he would not deviate from those answers ever... not once... not at all... not even a little bit... never...period... **DAMMIT!**

The age of miracles is still with us. Fred walked out of his Parole Officer's office that day under his own power and on his own recognizance and remains that way today!

Dan felt that a new light had dawned in the eternal darkness for those who are unable to answer successfully under duress without adult supervision. He suggested I add the information about the Drop-Down Answers to this book. It seemed like a good idea at the time.

Klutz as told by my son, Travis

By the time I was twelve years old I had begun to realize that I had an amazing ability to knock things over, even if I wasn't close to them. I can even do it from across the room when I'm in mid-season form. It's a sort of a gift, I suppose. Maybe with some training I could turn it into a short magic show or get my own page in the next *Ripleys' Believe It or Not.*

I used to yell and scream and cuss when I spilled something. At some point I began to laugh at my spill-ability and it has afforded me much mirth since then.

The first realization that I had this unique talent occurred to me one afternoon when I was a freshman in high school. I was on the phone (prior to the invention of cordless) and was wandering around the room, talking and trying desperately to come up with something cool to say to the young lady on the other end of the line. I was out for the Christmas Holidays and had just poured a big glass of eggnog. Knowing I was untrustworthy to carry a liquid and conversate on the phone simultaneously, I had judiciously placed the large glass of holiday cheer on a table.

You've guessed it! As I walked and talked, the cord from the phone ensnared the eggnog's glass and tumbled it over onto my mother's favorite dark blue carpet.

Today I just drink from containers with tightly secured lids and still I spill occasionally. I haven't demoted myself to a "sippey cup" yet but the thought has crossed my mind. I wonder if they make one big enough to hold a full liter of soda.

I rarely spill water. It's too easy to clean up and almost never leaves a permanent stain. I like to specialize in pigment heavy liquids like cherry Koolaid over a cream colored living room carpet.

It would be a waste of time and talent for me to spill coffee on the carpet in my dad's SUV. He ordered it with tan (coffee colored) carpeting in my honor.

My own personal vehicle is a pickup truck with no carpeting and no floor mats. I can, and do, just take a garden hose and slosh it out every few days.

The most recent expression of my gift involved our youngest cat. The cat infestation in our home is currently down to two from a recent high of five and the untrained observer might incorrectly assume that the cat-related accident quotient had dropped proportionately.

I'm an iced tea addict and keep a full glass by my bed at all times. Sometimes I even take a sip or two during the night to ward off the withdrawal symptoms. My tea glass rests on a twice folded paper towel on my bedside table beside my current paperback novel and a few treasured comics.

My youngest cat is a bug chaser: spiders, mosquitos, flies, anything small and mobile. One sunny afternoon she appeared in the living room sopping wet. I captured her and immediately realized she was not wet with water. That would have been too easy. She was soaked with heavily sugared iced tea.

I raced into the bedroom to find what you must by now expect, a messy bedside table and newly stained carpet. I don't know if the bug escaped or not.

Addendum by Scott:

I asked my grandson's mother as we sat at dinner how much milk to pour for five-year old Jackson. She replied with wisdom born of experience, "However much you feel like wiping up."

I suppose this kind of gift may have a genetic component.

Reunion

I graduated from High School in Atlanta, Georgia a long time ago and last spring I got an invitation to attend the 50th class reunion. I almost didn't go but my wife finally convinced me that I would have more hair and less tummy than most of the other guys; so I went.

I guess none of us look much like our senior pictures and I couldn't remember some of them even with the help of the Annual. At the Friday night open bar a classmate I sort of remembered named Roy bellied up next to me wearing a University of Georgia ball cap over an ill-fitting suit and started a conversation. He kind of reminded me of an unmade king sized bed. We chewed the usual fat. Where have you been, are you married, any kids, retired yet…and got reacquainted.

A few drinks later he asked me what I was doing the next morning. The next scheduled activity was the dance Saturday night. "Nothing," I replied naively unaware of the quicksand ahead.

He became most excited, "Meet me at the restaurant downstairs for breakfast at 7 and I'll take you out to my chicken farm."

Trapped! I had already admitted to having nothing else to do so all of the exits were blocked. This event is where I learned to answer such questions with a question such as, "What did you have in mind?" But I hadn't learned this technique yet so I was hooked.

Point of order in case you didn't know: a chicken farm is different from a chicken ranch.

I'm told that experience is what you get when you don't get what you want. I guess so because I was about to get some experience.

The next AM we drove about two hours northwest past civilization's last outpost in Georgia and finally arrived at our destination, appropriately enough at the end of a dirt road. There standing in all of its glory was a World War II Quonset hut the size of a battleship. It was a grey corrugated half-round aluminum pipe about twenty feet tall.

I thought, *How can it possibly get any better than a guided tour of this?*

Stay tuned for the answer.

The odor was curling my nose hairs and the commotion from the Quonset hut was so loud that I could hear it before we opened the car doors. My alleged friend handed me a pair of ear plugs. "You may want to wear these."

Yes, I thought, *I may want to kill you right now, too.*

Some of my readers, not being from the South, may not know that, "He needed killin'," is still a viable defense for a Murder One charge in the rural counties in most Southern States.

My (I almost said "friend") tormentor continued, "You're in luck. Today is the day we bring in the roosters to aaaah service the accounts... for lack of a better term. There's ten thousand chickens in there and my foreman just released the two hundred roosters. That's why it's so noisy."

Well, I'm not a great mathematician but I can run the numbers on that in my head. "You're going to be quite a few roosters short, aren't you?"

He responded, "Not too many years ago that would have been true. A good rooster could service about ten hens a day but one of the feed manufacturers has been working on vitamin and mineral enriched rooster food, and it's kinda expensive, but now a good rooster can service fifty or better in a single day."

I was impressed, "What's in that feed?"

"I don't know," he said, "but I can tell you it tastes terrible!"

Shockingly Beautiful Azaleas

My friend Patterson was in his early sixties back
when I hadn't yet found out how old "young" was
going to get. Young seems to me like it gets a bit
older every year.

He was spry and quite active for a man his age but by
his own admission was a lousy gardener. He had
what he called a black thumb. The only thing he was
ever able to grow with any success at all was
Azaleas.

His Azalea bushes started on the east side of his
house near the back and ran all the way down that
side, across the front, around the corner, and all the
way to the back on the west side. When they bloomed
each Spring his house looked like it had been built in
the middle of a rainbow. His bushes bloomed in
every color imaginable and he had interspersed white
ones to separate the various other colors.

After the Spring bloom, the Azaleas exploded with
tons of small green leaves, making a nice thick hedge
most of the way around the house. Patterson was very
proud of his Azaleas.

One Spring day he noticed that several of the bushes
on the southwest corner of the house had died. He
rushed down to the nursery and procured
replacements. A few weeks later the replacements
died so he replaced again.

He was on the way to meet me for an early morning fishing expedition about oh five thirty on an April Saturday when he heard his west side neighbors' front door open and close. As Patterson loaded his rods into the car he spotted his neighbor's boxer dog, Hercules wetting the Azaleas he had twice replaced.

Hercules had the typical Boxer dog's face and he slobbered a lot. If you were in range he would slime you when he shook his head. His looks and his behavior suggested that he just might have had several episodes of chasing parked cars.

Being a southern gentleman by birth and by nature, Patterson resisted the urge to use some Glock therapy on the dog and instead knocked on the neighbor's door. He calmly, according to Patterson, explained what was happening and asked his neighbor to modify Hercules' toilet habits to exclude the Azaleas. The neighbor agreed.

Unfortunately for the boxer dog, the man only agreed in word, not in deed. Patterson, being a suspicious chap, arose earlier than usual every day for the next week to patrol the bushes and on several occasions ran the dog off. He once again secured the neighbor's verbal commitment to revise the boxer's morning ritual; all to no avail.

On Friday afternoon, having run the dog off again that morning, Patterson committed himself to a major escalation in the battle to defend his beloved Azaleas. He worked at a hardware wholesale warehouse and one of the products his company carried was a fence electrifier designed to keep a 1500 pound bull from touching the fence…don't get ahead of me.

The fence electrifier can be used to electrify anything made of metal as it modifies the current so it hurts a bunch but doesn't do any permanent damage. He also acquired a bale of chicken wire and an extension cord…I told you not to get ahead of me.

Under cover of darkness, Patterson enclosed his precious Azaleas in chicken wire, connected the fence charger to the chicken wire and ran the extension cord from the charger to the front porch. He didn't want to leave it "hot" all night for fear that the local kids who were playing hide-and-seek might accidentally get shocked.

Patterson was on the front porch reading the paper and drinking coffee the next morning at oh five hundred when he heard the telltale sound of his neighbor's front door. Patterson reached down and plugged in the extension cord.

The boxer dog trotted over to his favorite bushes, assumed what football players refer to as the three point stance, and let fly.

Patterson reports that what came out of that boxer dog was the terribleist sound he'd ever heard. That electric shock didn't explode the dog's bladder but he probably thought it had.

They lived up on a hill with a view of a goodly distance in all directions and Patterson used to shield his eyes like his hand was the bill of a baseball cap when he told this part of the story. He said that the most amazing thing was that three blocks later, that boxer dog was still accelerating.

Taxidermy

My best friend, Ron used to own a small sporting goods store. I liked to hang around there when I had some spare time to drink free coffee and aggravate him with stories like this one. The only firm rule I had when in that establishment was that I would never help in any way.

He used to open around noon on Sundays in the Spring and Summer to catch the after church trade. There was a department store next door and many a man escaped a wifely shopping trip by telling his bride, "Go ahead on into the department store and start shopping, Honey. I'll catch up with you in a very few minutes. I promised Ron I'd check out a new fishing lure for him. You know that he considers me to be the best fisherman in this part of the country so I really need to try to help him when I can."

Then he'd come in and conceal himself in the back room for a while. Ron finally put some chairs back there by the TV so the truant husbands could hide more comfortably while they watched the ballgame.

One Sunday a little after twelve, while Ron was waiting on an actual customer, not a department store escapee, the prototypical little old lady came into the store. She was dressed in a lavender church outfit with those low high-heel shoes the matronly types seem to favor and was crowned with a lavender beret complete with veil. Ron looked up from his customer and greeted her, "Please make yourself at home,

Ma'am. I'll be with you as soon as I finish with this gentleman."

Ron was an easy grader when it came to the title, "gentleman". He was working with our friend Darrin Jay who had been called a lot of things in his life but gentleman certainly wasn't one of them. When Ron was on best behavior he threw "gentleman" and other polite terms around like Frisbees.

The lady turned around just inside the door and looked up at a deer head that guarded the entrance. I believe it was a ten pointer. She studied it for a few moments and then started down the far aisle. A few steps later she stopped to inspect a largemouth bass that was hanging just above head level over the fish hook display. A little further on she stopped and examined a very life like raccoon that Ron's taxidermist had displayed on a branch over the pocket knives.

Ron is usually as sharp as a warm marshmallow but none of the lady's actions were lost on him that day.

When he finished with the other customer Ron approached the lady, "Can I help you with something today, Ma'am?"

She smiled as she looked up over her half glasses and spoke in a soft voice, "Well I hope so, Sonny. You see, I've had these two bunny rabbits for the longest time. They were a married couple, if you know what I mean and all of the neighborhood children just loved them. The kids helped me by feeding them and cleaning out the bunny hutch and some of them even got to witness the miracle of birth there."

She took a breath and her expression saddened, "I came out to feed the rabbits this morning before church and they were both just lying there on the bottom of the cage. They must have died during the night."

Ron is not a quick study as I have mentioned before but he was sure he was reading this one correctly when he asked, "Would you like to have them mounted?"

"No," she replied, "I think maybe just holding hands."

Language of the Heart

My friend and I spent a day in downtown Tokyo in a district known as the Ginza. It was replete with restaurants, shops and department stores. He and I wandered into an upscale department store around 4 PM. We were immediately struck by how clean everything was. The floors were spotless and on either side of the up escalator were two young ladies in uniforms, each holding a neatly folded white handkerchief on the rail as it slid by. They were wiping the rail.

We wandered up a floor at a time, exploring and eventually found ourselves on the roof. It was a miniature amusement park complete with a small train, several food vendors and an assortment of games somewhat similar to our pinball machines but considerably smaller. Apparently the custom was for ladies of means to drop their children off on the roof with a pocket full of ten yen coins, worth about three cents each, and then, when they finished shopping retrieve the children.

Scattered about the roof were about twenty-five children, all in school uniforms, and ranging from seven years old to about twelve.

Jerry and I approached the first game machine and I put in a coin. Things I did not understand began to happen inside the mechanism. I assume I not only lost but posted the record low score. We laughed and moved to the next one, quickly creating a similar result but by that time we had drawn a small crowd.

"Why are they staring at us?" I asked my friend.

"We have funny eyes," he replied, "and we clearly have no idea what we're doing."

One of the bravest of our small audience approached us and pointed to a machine for us to watch. He inserted a coin and successfully played the machine. It was shaped like a pinball machine and it spit marble sized steel balls at a fast rate. The balls rolled down toward the player, bouncing off of various bumpers. Inside the glass at the bottom was a four inch square catching device that the player could move left and right by spinning a wheel that protruded from the near side of the machine's cabinet. Apparently the object was to catch as many balls as possible.

Jerry took a turn after the boy and did much better than he had without instruction.

By this time all of the roof-bound kids were gathered noisily around us. He and I made great displays of exuberance when we did anything right or wrong in a game to gales of laughter from our spectators. It was a magical scene as we moved from machine to machine.

Suddenly the faces of our assembled throng all dropped at once. They all stared blankly at the floor and a heavy silence immediately replaced the cacophony. Something awful had apparently just happened and we had no idea what. I assumed one of us had inadvertently made a major social blunder.

We found out as we approached the next game. It was a boxing game. There was a two dimensional boxer with a three dimensional nose that bobbed and weaved behind the vertical glass at the back of the machine. A handle stuck up out of the top of the machine near the player and slamming it forward would cause a boxing glove on an armature to punch at the fighter. The object was to hit the nose.

The boxer was obviously a Caucasian and our young friends were clearly concerned that we'd be offended or hurt. We were not. Jerry dropped a coin in and started swinging away. As I cheered our young friends joined in and joy was restored.

An hour later we bought a round of ice cream to top off the day.

That afternoon has had a profound effect on me. I am convinced that a loving God watches over all of us, His children, and one of my assignments is to learn to love all of us, without exception. I began to understand that lesson at the hands of some Japanese children that day; children who thought I had funny eyes.

We spoke no Japanese and they spoke no English but we all spoke Fun, Ice Cream and Laughter which I now think of as the Language of the Heart.

ACKNOLWEDGEMENTS

I'd like to thank Ron Fielder who is really my co-author or accomplice depending on your perspective. He was heavily involved in creating many of the lies and a few of the true stories. I also accused him of a number of things of which he is possibly innocent.

Thanks to Darrin Jay Morrissey for allowing me to use his name and characteristics to create a couple of my characters and to Will Dempsey for allowing me to tell the truth about him and for being my computer mentor.

Thanks to John Edmonds without whose support and advice this would have not been completed and to Jean Noell without whose motivation I might never have finished.

Thanks also to Sherry Bohannon for a badly needed edit.

Thanks to my son, Travis for *Klutz* and for a fine edit.

Thanks to Wall Street Dan Schweihs for providing a place to write and for the Drop-Down Answers.

Thanks to Chuck Phipps who stars in ***Charity*** and is one of my heroes.

Thanks to my former wife, Linda for several very funny ideas.

Thanks to Dale Goodloe who did his usual amazing work on the cover.

I would like to give special thanks to several close friends for helping me through a very difficult time in my life. You know who you are and I cannot thank you enough.

Other Books by Scott Lee

Spirituality for the Religiously Challenged: Schoolhouse Earth Books Volume I

This book is a set of spiritual observations, activities and lessons on developing a fun, productive and effective spiritually based life. These easy to follow directions will bring you a new joy, no matter what your religious beliefs are. They are especially effective for those who do not have a religion or a spiritual connection at all.

ISBN 978-1478147862

Salesmen Can Go to Heaven: Schoolhouse Earth Books Volume II

Acquire an honest spiritual approach to the world of sales. Learn to make a good living selling while remaining true to the Spiritual Principles that guide the universe. This book has been authorized to and contains a full description and history of John Steinhouse's innovative concept, The Extilliation Factor.

ISBN 978-1478160281

Stop Smoking the Hard Way: Schoolhouse Earth Books Volume III

If one of the easy ways to quit smoking had worked, you would not be reading this! Learn a simple spiritually based method for becoming a non-smoker. Being religious is not a requirement as anyone with an open mind can use it effectively. Smoking is both addiction and habit. This groundbreaking method

eradicates the habit first. When the habit is gone the addiction is much easier to break.
ISBN 978-1478160403

All Schoolhouse Earth Books are based on the premise that Earth is a school and that I got here by flunking out of somewhere else or I was expelled as a behavior problem.

All three of these are available from Amazon.com and from Createspace.com

The following books are in progress and I hope to publish them in the near future:

Grandparenting Kindergarten
Learn ideas, games, meal planning, field trips and other tips on how to become your grandchildren's favorite toy. Also pick up useful hints on how to get maximum enjoyment for yourself from your time with your Grandchildren. Using these techniques you will be smiling when they arrive and still smiling when they depart. If you only pick up one idea that makes you a better grandparent, this book will be well worth your while.

Conquering The Old Lies That Are Running Your Life
This is the working title of a non-fiction book. The core Old Lie is that I'm not good enough and if you folks could see the real me, not the act I'm presenting to you most of the time, you wouldn't want me around. This book uncovers the source of the Old Lies and presents an easy to follow procedure for

conquering those Old Lies and changing the behaviors the Old Lies created.

Conversations with an Alien
This is the working title of a science fiction, or maybe a science non-fiction book that is based on the fact that beings from other planets regularly visit planet Earth. Many of my pilot friends have seen them. It answers the questions: Why don't they communicate with us? What do they want here? Come visit with our alien friend "Tom" as he answers these and many more questions. He also explains why Earth is the laughing stock of the galaxy and what we must do to join the galactic community.

True Flying Stories and Other Lies Volume 1
This series of short stories is based on my experience as a pilot for the United States Air Force from 1967 to 1971. It will take you from brake release to 40,000 feet in three and a half minutes; fly you through a sand storm at thirty-three thousand feet; show you the curvature of the Earth; land on the Greenland ice cap; and present a series of practical jokes that flyers like to play on each other.

We are actively seeking contributors to *True Flying Stories and Other Lies Volume 1* and to *True Fish Stories and Other Lies Volume 2.*

If you would like to contribute, please email me at: Scott@SchoolhouseEarthBooks.com

About the Author

A Fisherman was born June 28, 1943 in Atlanta, Georgia and his name is Scott Jackson Lee. He is a 1966 graduate of The University of the South, Sewanee, Tennessee and a 1967 graduate of United States Air Force Pilot Training. He had the honor and privilege of piloting 7 different types of military aircraft for 5 years and 2000 hours.

Today he lives in Nashville, Tennessee where he is currently writing *TRUE FLYING STORIES AND OTHER LIES: VOLUME 1* as well as *TRUE FISH STORIES AND OTHER LIES: Volume 2*.